GRANDCHILDREN
AND OTHER POEMS

BY

BERNARD KOPS

Hearing Eye

Published by
Hearing Eye,
Box 1,
99 Torriano Avenue,
London NW5 2RX

COPYRIGHT © Bernard Kops 2000

ISBN 1 870841 69 7

This publication has been made possible with the financial
assistance of the London Arts Board.

Printed by Aldgate Press, London E1
Typeset by Daniel James at mondo designo

INSPIRED BY AND DEDICATED TO
ERICA AND THE TRIBE

CONTENTS

POEMS ARE LIKE GRANDCHILDREN

Poems are like grandchildren
you should never bribe or persuade them
to visit you.
They must turn up of their own accord
and when their faces light up your
eyes
you should never rush to embrace them
at the open door
but wait until they enter and overwhelm
and delight you.
Never ask will you stay?
They may well need to rush away.

Poems are like grandchildren
they come close in their own good time.

JESSICA BORN

From the deserts of dark,
someone came to this oasis,
hungry for the milk of stars.
Given a name,
she now sleeps at the breast
of my daughter,
a piece of dreaming
sculpture.

Pale and perfect,
only her mouth moves,
sucking sunlight.
The night dies.

Then suddenly she is becoming,
stirring, opening eyes.
And all at once she is alive,
is one of us.
She cries and cries.

You have to laugh.

JESSICA TWO

She runs around the room with nothing on
I coax her into socks with silly songs.
Big Girls always put on clothes.
She cries when I suggest she now wears shoes
and rushes to the window, points at sky,
Look Grandpa I'm a bird; and I can fly.
I can fly higher than the sky;

All you have to do is wind me up.

JESSICA NEARLY THREE

You sing in your doll's-house;
chatting to no-one,
oblivious to us.
Lucky you.
Stay there as long as possible.
There is nothing here
that we can offer,
except greed and chaos.
And sadness.
Your dolls do not queue in the supermarket.
They do not see their fraught reflections
at the Checkout. How angry they have become.
How quietly mad they have gone; how tragic,
how despairing, trundling home with baskets full
of empty lives.
Your dolls do not pass the young old,
sleeping on pavements, unloved,
unloving.
They belong.
They are valued in your universe.

You play in your doll's-house,
unaware of the Medusa on the box,
with her head of snakes;
her Ministers;
who hiss their sweet venom, their arrogance.
so that we too fall sick, pass on their contagion.

This is not Rome of the crucifixions.
Not Egypt of the Pharaohs,
Nor Babylon.
Nor the Black Death of the Middle Ages.
This is Britain, 1988.
Granddaughter these are the Dark Ages.
Yet you remain unaware.
Immune to all this desperation.
Stay in your Doll's-house.
All your invisible friends have come for tea.
And your laughter falls like golden rain,
reminding us there is more than greed
more than pain.
I pray that by the time you understand these words
the plague will have passed,
and the world and you can emerge out of darkness.

JESSICA THREE

Your laughter a waterfall in a desert of traffic jams.
Don't grow.
Don't grow and go to school.
They will cram your head with garbage,
pluck the joy right out of your eyes.
What will they teach you that
you do not know?
That you must love and be loved?
No!
They will shove numbers into your head
They will numb you and blind you with the science
of their survival.
They will teach you how to eat your friends
as well as your foe.

They will fix you
At eight you will be talking of security, mortgages,
pensions.
At nine endowment policies, shares
At ten they will teach you how to own the world.
You will be old so soon.
You will forget how to sing;
once they get their claws into you.
Climb the climbing frame!
swing upside down
Cartwheel. Be a disgrace. Cover your face and dress with
such unholy mess. Roll on the grass
Scream and love yourself
Dance under the moon.
Flout your nakedness;
astonish every house,
shout with wonder, joy,
when you suddenly notice stars.
Don't go! Stay where you are.
Stay three.
And run towards me
holding wide your arms,
laughing like the end of this world.

MAX ARRIVES

Weeks before he was born they named him.
Names come from deserts, from families,
from ancestors; from dreams, hopes, aspirations.
Names cement these tenuous skeins
of flesh into a living person,
someone who belongs, and will ignite
the fire, hurl it onward.
The night before he came through the door,
my daughter, floating in the waters of time
laughed and cried.
Between these two shores all beings
will negotiate the parapet of life.
Her partner supplied the flowers
of encouragement, gentle words of strength
to bring the thing about.
Whereupon she pushed him out
of his ocean home, to provide another home
here in this world.
Max! Name of new being.
Named after him, the great grandfather long dead;
the old man who slipped back
into the universe, gently, without much
complaining
a million years ago, or ten.
In death all time is timeless.
In birth he was suddenly here, this new being.
A silver milky globule, demanding, ravenous for life.
For weeks now I have tried to write these words.
This fanfare, announcing him was expected of me.
But what are words compared to a human child?
A new life?
Yet in the night I awoke, suddenly
and had no fear to approach this impossible mountain.

Aware of my heartbeat I entered myself,
where half ushered, slouching in a corner
of a corridor were my words. These old men
did not speak to each other.
Shy in their own shadow.
Afraid of assassination, of being uttered.
Each word of unformed Golem
afraid to sing of this birth of my new grandson,
for fear they would not be adequate
against the greater miracle of being.
On this ledge of eternity,
I touch them, bang their heads together.
I beg, threaten. I plead with them.
Cry, pray. I bring them all together,
and then I sing them.
Max is my immortality.
The one who went before and who will come after;
who soon will banish the dark with laughter.
And I want to sing for him before I go back to sleep.

It's morning. Suddenly sunshine.
And he is here and this is here. And so am I.
Birdsong!

MAX TEN MONTHS OLD

London. Winter. Time running out for this lost world.
How will we survive these virtual festivities?
Wet penetrating rain the only reality.
No-one will boldly come to seek us out and save us.
We are the voyeurs, running up the down staircase.
We celebrate this shortest day
searching, deifying Pagan godlings. Going plastic mad.
The fag end of the year.
Christmas. Goodwill to all men.
So what about women? No wonder they smile knives,
murder lurking in their knowing eyes.
Thank god we may not slide into the earth without screaming.
Christ mass! That's all we need.
How will we survive their saviour? How will we survive
these latter days? By stuffing ourselves for comrade worm?
Nietzsche said God is dead. I'm not feeling too well myself.
Friends explode. Relatives implode. The sky closes down.
Dark closes in.
Skeletons haggle over bankrupt stock in Oxford Street.
Halleluiah! Season of goodcheer for the undead.
Rabbis, priests lurk in doorway, practising popsongs.
Let's face it, we need a package deal to somewhere else.
Sweatless desperation.
Tubed. Work. Home to mortgage box. We come in
we pace for a while, then we go out.
All in all we needn't have been here.
You could say we've had it. It's too late.
But wait? See the one glimmer on the horizon.
There! In the afternoon my grandson Max!
Ten months old, claps his hands
kisses a moment of golden sun.
And all the darkness of doubt
and all the questions

and all the answers have no meaning.
And the universe and all the cosmic winds
of winter and the chill of endless night
ignite in a puff of laughter.
He lights up the sky.

MAX AND THE MEANING OF LIFE

Max and the meaning of life?
To understand the mystery of
nights and days
I need look no further than my
daughter Hannah,
and the child she cradles with
her gaze.
He came through the door
to prove that it was there, the
door that leads to dreams,
restoring all our hope,
allowing us to dare, to believe
there's more than earth.

Max came out of the dark, his life a golden spark.
rising from the dark, singing in the park,
His father's name is Mark.

So suddenly he came. Shooting the rapids of time,
the avalanche of space.
I stare into his face.
This miracle of love; this traveller unlost
sculptured by centuries of cosmic dust.
Still tangled in the skein of womb; the mystery of love.
This Cosmic Child just born. He stares back from the
dark;
from centuries of space.
And when I search his face there's Shiva in her dance
with Adam in his trance. In life we take a chance
And try to make a shape.
And laugh and dare to hope
and so enhance our days, whilst we are here on earth.

New birth brings new life
and life in us is reborn.
His being is answered prayer.
Deliverance from endless stare.
Of gazing in the glass.
Is there anyone out there?
Is there anyone in there
who can guide us through the dark?

His being is my prayer; this Max so suddenly ours.
He proves the door is there.
There beyond our stare; our arrow through the
stars.

SNAPSHOT OF ANYA

...and Anya upside down, pointing at the window
and laughing. Then tumbling, mumbling
in that lost language
the Esperanto of one year on earth,
between rage and kisses
insisting that we too
watch the silver moon in the cobalt sky
slowly progressing across the bare black branches

ANYA

Throwing me a smile, a crumb of charity
she runs away.
when I open my arms for her embrace
she teases, pouts a kiss
calls my name, coming close.
touching me with her fingertips.
I reach out, I dare to hope she's becoming
compassionate, almost human.

I should have known better
learned to play the same game
she has so perfected.
But when you lose your heart
you lose your head.
And I have lost my heart forever
to a heartless one
an angel of sheer delight.
I make one final plea
for reason
No use.

Nothing is fair
in the fairground of the heart.

She runs circles around me
giggling, teasing.
And I give in. I surrender
The general is defeated.
He looks up to the sky, wounded, smiling
wondering how and when and why
he lost this war.
As she rides away, away
on her rocking horse.

CHLOE

Out of the darkness of nothing
she arrived
pulling into this harbour
the shores of West Hampstead
as if not terrified
of the millions of aeons
that surrounded her journey
to us
She came by way of Diaspora Umbilica
taking in the songs and sorrows
of Odessa
the cries of Riga, Amsterdam
the sighs of Dublin
the winds of Dartmoor
And now she manages to sit up
with such delight
holding out her arms, staking her claim
to all of us with smiles.

THREE IN THE MORNING

Looking at photographs
there is one face in the darkness
one recurring image
Erica throwing flowers over her shoulder
high into that black sky

I think often of nothingness
and the fear, the chill at three in the morning
of the absurdity of being and not being

those Irises
that purple explosion in that winter of poverty
when we lived on laughter

maybe this is my raft into the hereafter.

FOUR IN THE MORNING

Going back to bed at four in the morning

Erica sleeping;
smiling as she surfs the dark waves of
all our ocean years, enclosed in this embrace

I laugh at all those who will wake believing today
will be different from yesterday

and at those who believe that today will be the
same as yesterday.

Going back to bed, the tightrope before dawn. The balancing act, vision of grandchildren, negotiating the chasm, the singing strand trembles, sometimes I soar and fall and find myself bouncing in the air and sleep images floating as I slowly motion my stance back in to the slow safety of cobalt skies.

Grandchildren so easily dance upon the wire. Anya the newest. I breathe in the smell of the universe.

She stands before she can crawl;
laughing when she falls.

How madly human we are. We deserve ourselves.

Oh the unbelievable beauty of this world. The music of being, of being Max the prince who will roam the cosmos, with his sword of stars... Grandson, your paths point in every direction, your embrace. Your breath. The sweet wonder of this world

and Jessica, our golden apple, daughter of daughter, you have me reaching for my heart and my pocket.

Living cantatas of spring, emissaries into the future, proving all this will still exist

always

and I can swim the cosmos and return to us.

ERICA BY LETHE

You wandered along the shore
considering the other side;
and I watched you, helpless.

There was nothing I could do
as I waited,
with all the nerve endings
of my love exposed;
unable, useless.
For the first time somehow at a loss.

You looked back at me,
your calm eyes floating above your pain,
as if weighing things up,
considering perhaps that I
would give you an even rougher ride
if you returned to us.

But it was for you to decide.

You chatted to the Boatman,
haggled for a while,
then suddenly you decided not to cross.

And so you came back to us, smiling.

1977

PEOPLE

People always reassure
that everything will turn out right
you thank them,
then you close the door,
and lie awake all night.

OPERATION

You'll be alright Erica said.
But darling I could end up dead.
Then, going down into the anaesthetic
universe I give a long drawn out sigh;
you know, the Esperanto of the Jewish World.
In return she gives birth to an incredible smile;
somehow that alone makes life worthwhile.

But as they wheel me away
through the door I cry
If you let me die I won't talk to you anymore.

THE ULTIMATE TRUTH

Parents carry photos of their children.
Children never carry photos of their parents

CHILDREN 1

Who are these strangers come within these walls,
who now are fast asleep?
Their hands do not seem to need
to grasp or guard;
but are opened upward, palms towards the stars.
Why are they surrendering
when they have captured us?

CHILDREN 2

Today the laughter of my daughter
was drowned in the sadness of my son.
He stood there on the shores of life
silent and lost in the labyrinth of his eyes.

And all the time ravenous winter
swallowed light and danced
with him.

Slowly and slowly
the cymbal clouds
clapped hands and he cried
and cried himself to sleep.

In the morning he emerged
laughing.

And my daughter sobbing
huddled under the blankets
in the pyramid of her grief.

DAUGHTER DAUGHTER

I'm sorry she said I really am
I nodded and mumbled and left the room
Didn't you hear? Are you that deaf?

And there in the garden I held my breath
and studied the flowers but she followed me out
and there in the garden she started to shout

I apologised what more do you want? What more do you want?
Say something or frown!
I really am sorry it was all my fault.

Good I replied, looking at the sky, keeping my head down.
Forget it my darling, you're overwrought
I whistled and smiled and walked away.
She stalked me and stalked me all that day.

I said I was sorry. I'm entirely to blame.
You don't really believe me
you're always the same.

Oh my daughter I know this game.
When children are sorry there is no doubt
they open the door for another bout.

MY SISTER PHYLLIS

You have gone.

Unexpectedly you went,
reminding us that we must go
without our consent.
You are gone,
are gone.

You had no choice,
yet still I hear your voice,
lingering.
Life trembles on the brink
of the dark,
and dark ignites from a single spark
of nothingness.

You have gone.
Your dust
sprinkled
in
the
earth.

Life is our love,
and our belonging,
and our longing your rebirth

WHITECHAPEL LIBRARY, ALDGATE EAST

How often I went in for warmth and a doze
The newspaper room whilst my world outside froze
And I took out my sardine sandwich feast.
Whitechapel Library, Aldgate East.
And the tramps and the madman and the chattering crone.
The smell of their farts could turn you to stone
But anywhere, anywhere was better than home.

The joy to escape from family and war.
But how can you have dreams?
you'll end up on the floor.
Be like your brothers, what else is life for?

You're lost and you're drifting, settle down, get a job.
Meet a nice Jewish girl, work hard, earn a few bob.
Get married, have kids; a nice home on the never
and save for the future and days of rough weather.

Come back down to earth, there is nothing more.
I listened and nodded, like I knew the score.
and early next morning I crept out the door.

Outside it was pouring.
I was leaving forever.

I was finally, irrevocably done with this scene,
The trap of my world in Stepney Green.
With nowhere to go and nothing to dream

A loner in love with words, but so lost
I wandered the streets, not counting the cost.

I emerged out of childhood with nowhere to hide.
when a door called my name
And pulled me inside.

And being so hungry I fell on the feast.
Whitechapel Library, Aldgate East.

And my brain explodes when I suddenly find
an orchard within for the heart and the mind.
The past was a mirage I'd left far behind

And I am a locust and I'm at a feast.
Whitechapel Library, Aldgate East.

And Rosenberg also came to get out of the cold
To write poems of fire, but he never grew old.
And here I met Chekov, Tolstoy, Meyerhold.
I entered their worlds, their dark visions of gold.

The reference library, where my thoughts were to
rage.
I ate book after book, page after page.
I scoffed poetry for breakfast and novels for tea.
And plays for my supper. No more poverty.
Welcome young poet, in here you are free
to follow your star to where you should be.

That door of the library was the door into me.

And Lorca and Shelley said "Come to the feast."
Whitechapel Library, Aldgate East.

THE DEAD GIRL

So many people come into our house
and go out.
Faces of friends; faces of relatives,
they rarely stay.
We prefer it that way.

She came into our house,
a perfect stranger.
She smiled, stayed for one hour
and then she was gone.

So many have come and gone, come and gone.
Their faces coagulate.

Why then do we think of her,
this unknown, lovely girl?

Because she is still there,
standing in a far dark corner,
watching us forever.

NEIGHBOUR

The woman suddenly became disturbed,
thought she was a ravenous bird.
She pecked at the mirror, at her other self,
then took her husband off the shelf.
She dusted him and asked his name.
He laughed until his eyes belched flame.
After love and liquid he gently said
what's going on inside your head?
She opened up, he looked inside,
then he committed suicide.

POOR OLD CROW

(Note from nature article. *"Crow parents almost work themselves to death trying to feed their voracious young".*)

I feel so close to crow.
I hover limp and ragged, croaking low.
I who sought the highest tree, so tired now;
I flap so slow. But I'll find the strength
to wave goodbye, for soon they'll go.

They'll leave poor crow,
poor thankful crow.
I'll sigh—Oh dear, must you go?
I'll cry.
I'll hide my wicked beady eye,
so full of glee.

I watch them practice flight,
day and night I hear them rise
and fall.
I've seen it all.
How terrible my children,
must you go? Must you leave old crow?

Oh soon I also want to go.
I want to fly away with lady crow,
I want some years of gluttony,
for me.

WINTER SPRINGSONG

Winter the heavy breather
won't let go.
Peeking through the window,
creaking through the floorboards,
coughing through the walls,
howling through the corridors,
wheezing through the dark,
tapping with his white stick.
The old swine won't let go.

Go winter go!

You dirty old man,
hobble off, away with you,
We've had quite enough.
Haven't you heard the news?
We're dancing in this room,
as naked as our love;
as cheering as our song,
as fervent as our eyes,
as singing as our limbs,
as crazy as our hope.
Creep into a corner,
die and wither there,
as clouds unclothe the sun.

WE FURNISH DREAMS
(FOR M.R.)

In this dream it is early morning.
We come to a familiar house.
The place where we live
The son of a poet has just died
absurdly young. He aspired to furnish dreams
But he stopped overnight
at a wayward place and decided
not to return.
His father, and his friend, my son in law
have brought him here.
I sit unmoved as they lift the coffin so easily,
as if the boy is filled with air,
out of the black taxi
and move backwards
in slow motion towards the house
to where these other children play
to prove they are still living
and therefore will not be thrown away.
They are meant to see the boy
for the last time.
With ease the young men carry the box
and strangely laughing
as if to celebrate a joyous event.
It all seems so appropriate.

I have always been scared
of the great giant fish;
with its ever gaping mouth
trawling the side streets for the old,
those neighbours who suddenly are gone
ever so quietly, unrecorded on video.
The children come outside into the inside

singing, dancing. Friends. Brothers.
Young sisters. And how they laugh.
Flying angels.
So far the ceremony has been in black and white
but when they lift off the lid
the whole scene bursts into colour.
From upstairs I can see the perfect
slight smiling face, absurdly young.
He does not struggle
against this exodus.
But somewhere deep in the house
that now isn't there,
I hear a young woman softly crying clouds.

Now all my grandchildren come, those born
and those not yet arrived.
They play football in the sudden street.
The great ball of fire goes sailing
through the sky.
Then I realise that I am in that box.
I am the stopped boy and I am carrying him.
I chuck away my wet smudged eyes.
I am his nodding, singing father, and myself.
I supply the colour, the faces, the houses.
The laughter, the sobbing mother.
I am his sisters, his brothers
getting on with their lives: their dreams.
I conjure Births and exits. Deaths
and entrances.
I furnish dreams.

An old man shuffles along the road.
I try to not catch up with him.
But he knows I am there,
and turns to me, smiling. "Don't grow old!"

He scythes. When he drops dead
I walk over him. He could have been my father.
I never etched his face.

I will never grow old.

In the world of waking, the world of true dreams,
where people are plucked so suddenly,
leaving leaves and debts and sky and
grandchildren, who will hug you
while lovers weep in a back room,
we have no choice.
It is still not such a bad place to furnish dreams.

The young men and their box are going now.
They are floating to a soft suburb to plant him there.

And when they drive away everyone cheers.
This is a dream, remember. We furnish dreams.

EXILE

It is raining outside,
It is raining.
The wet leaves are rotting into the earth,
into the sockets of my father's song,
into the mouth of my mother's skull
where she smiles for all eternity.

I am clutched by a cold sadness,
by loneliness, by loss.
Where do I belong?
I feel far away.
But far away from where?

It is raining outside;
far away from the wind on the hills
of my dream,
from the pipes and the birds of my song.

My son laughs in a strange language,
a language I understand too well.

Perhaps I should take my life and death
with me,
walk with my wife and my son and two
blankets,
into the rain.

1964

FOR ADAM

My son, I have brought you into this;
into this world.
And I have never thought but loved.
Yet had I thought I would have done the same,
and I would never have you unborn,
and I have always loved your name,
since I threw my flame into another flame
and held you weeping when you came.

A girl and I and one night loving
dreamed and dredged you from the stars,
and up you came.
I loved your mother, and I love her,
and I put you into her,
and now my love for her walks with you.

So be gentle in the night.

It is customary my son to tell you things;
to show you the way.
I who am lost and burning and trembling in the dark.

These words then are instead of words,
instead of tears.

So there you are; here.
Survivor from the night,
refugee from space. Smoke you are,
taken shape.
Beautiful child in the ghetto of of your mind,
lost within the congregation of your shadows.

My son! You have your head, your heart, your soul,
your name, your fears, your face,

No-one can die your death or live your life.
We see you trying to take your place,
and search the questions that cloud your face,
we hear you singing with the worm,
we watch you struggling to conform.

And though your tears tear us apart
somewhere we are glad.

They can swim my son.
They can negotiate roads and sky and water
and rooms packed with people.
Falling in the garden does not cause them to drown.

Out of the window I see you all alone,
pursued by all of them.
But they do not see that your are pursued
by all the aeroplanes from within.
They do not hear your singing rabbis weeping
centuries of psalm and dust.
They do not smell these fearful faces of the past
who haunt you,
that cause the tears to fall along your lovely head.

Take care. Go through your way and come out
as you shall.
Out of your shell of troubled sleep.

I sing of the times when these words have no meaning,
of a girl and you and one night loving;
who dream and dredge me up from dark.
Until then I hail you in your hell.
Become familiar with the stations of the star
so that you may truly enter out of pain.

And try to smile.

PRAYER AT FORTY

There is this noise of silence
as I enter my house;
and these children in attitudes
of praying stone.
I cover them and they moan.

And there is this woman
in this room,
the girl who took my name
and breathed upon it.
There is this warm in my bed
when I touch and kiss her sleeping form.

There is this you, miracled in the mirror.

I will go to bed.
I will close my head
and enter the dark flower of my wife.

You are a mirage in this desert.
I have drunk from you, sang songs beneath your cool limbs.

I climb into bed.

I had grown old wandering in this desert.
My tongue had got thick and had gone mad and cursed God.
And I died.

But now I sing of marriage;
of love and work and marriage,
for only these exist.

Somewhere upon these impossible stairs
we are attempting love.
And the fire from our eyes may burn
down this city.
For let us face it,
all in all we remain unearthed in North West Six.

Tomorrow we must wear disguise
and cry in tubes and turn away
from mumbled lives and the dumb
articulation of passers-by.

Dreaming one. Do you remember grass?
And walking through the orchards
of this metropolis?
Our children will soon awake.
Already I can hear the singing bird
in this black night.

They will rise and go up
into the Jerusalem of tomorrow;
into the unborn lemon city of the heart;
into the soaring of arrows, the gathering
of flowers, and bread.

They must go up with their open eyes,
climbing the dust pyramids of our dead;
and reach high enough to see
the fresh grass that breathes beyond,
and the unsmashed glass, and you and I.
And the bird with sun on throat and wing.

The limbs and the love and the laugh
of our children must go up and never die.

And we all will sing.

QUESTIONS

What does your father do?
What does he do for a living?

He is a decomposer,
and his eyes are open,
twenty four hours of every, every day.

What does your mother do?
What does she do for a living?

She is an earthwife.
And she lies beside him
forever and ever,
and ever.

HALL OF MIRRORS

He came for me tonight with shooting stars,
he came towards me in the dark firing crimson grass.

I love you my brother, creeping through the dark.
I wait for you to hurl the flash and chant the black.

He came for me tonight and sang the trees.
Into the hall of mirrors he scattered eyes.
We elongate, distend and try to pray
and point and grimace, laugh; then blend and sway
into the passage of our father's psalm.
And end our dream of days and shattered glass.

Shattered glass always figures in my dreams,
in this hall of mirrors where I wait for him.

I wait for him to roll me up in earth,
to take me to the ocean made of mother's tears.

PASSOVER '38

One thing I remember
even more than the hunger.
Scrubbing my knees, smarting my hair and
rushing downstairs
into that playground of my childhood;
where all the other children
with their eyes alight
were building castles with crackernuts.

I built my castle.
I was a shopkeeper, a millionaire,
I ruled the world;
challenging all to chance
nuts of their own,
gathered from high pitched aunts
the day before,
as we went from home to home,
running that Yomtov gauntlet
of twisted cheeks and wet kisses.

In those days families extended forever and ever.

Who wants a castle?
Knock down my castle! I dared.
All in their sudden beauty
the girls came singing, flirting.
Holiday! Passover!
The Angel of Death? Who is he?
a madman on the radio, far away.

Passover lasted for the rest of the year;
the crackernuts secure
in the lining of my sleeve.
Belonging — we belonged.

Poverty came later,
when most of us did well
and moved away.

BREAKDOWN

All night I dreamed I lay awake,
and now the day goes rushing through.
Borrowed from darkness once again,
I find that I have lost myself.

I leave a small note on the table.
Dear Mum, O can U not C how ill I am?
Goodbye.

I rush out through the wallpaper
and walk along the crowded parchment.

Help! Help! Catch me, I'm falling. Hell—
Childcall, birdflight, down to the endless seas
of the never ending, ending night.

The sediment of dusk falls,
into the husk of night.

A spider sleeps and dreams of silver.

Oh, we are the fragments of a dream,
a dream that has no dreamer.

BARRICADES IN WEST HAMPSTEAD

All my children talk to me.
More or less.
And I have loved the same woman
for forty five years.
I suppose you could call that success,
if you ignore the pain
of almost everything.
And what's more we've been together
and stayed sane.
More or less.
Yes!
Despite the encroaching endless mess;
the heartless conversions
that threaten to engulf West Hampstead,
I still maintain my ridiculous oasis.
And here sometimes even neighbours
manage to smile and nod.
And my granddaughter thinks that I am god.
Why am I such a lucky sod?
More or less.

SHALOM BOMB

I want a bomb, my own private bomb, my shalom bomb.
I'll test it in the morning, when my son awakes,
hot and stretching, smelling beautiful from sleep. Boom! Boom!

Come my son dance naked in the room.
I'll test it on the landing and wake my neighbours,
the masons and the whores and the students who live down-stairs.

Oh I must have a bomb and I'll throw open windows and
count down as I whizz around the living room,
on his bike, with him flying angels on my shoulder;
and my wife dancing in her dressing gown.
I want a happy family bomb, a do-it-yourself bomb,
I'll climb on the roof and ignite it there about noon.
My improved design will gong the world and we'll all eat lunch.

My pretty little bomb will play a daytime lullaby and
thank you bomb for now my son falls fast asleep.
My love come close, close the curtains, my lovely bomb, my
darling.

My naughty bomb. Burst around us, burst between us, burst within us.

Light up the universe, then linger, linger
while the drone of the world recedes.

Shalom bomb

I want to explode the breasts of my wife,
and wake everyone,
to explode over playgrounds and parks, just as children
come from schools. I want a laughter bomb,
filled with sherbert fountains, licorice allsorts, chocolate kisses, candy floss,

tinsel and streamers, balloons and fireworks, lucky bags,
bubbles and masks and false noses.

I want my bomb to sprinkle the earth with roses.
I want a one-man-band-bomb. My own bomb.

My live long and die happy bomb. My die peacefully of old age bomb,
in my own bed bomb.
My Om Mane Padme Aum Bomb, My Tiddly Om Pom Bomb.
My goodnight bomb, my sleeptight bomb,
my see you in the morning bomb.
I want my bomb, my own private bomb, my Shalom bomb.

DANCING PARTNER

Our forty years have just sailed by;
we dance and watch them come and go.
So lean on me and give me strength
and I'll forgive you all my sins.

OUR KIDS HAVE JUST LEFT HOME

We sit here rather dazed:
our kids have just left home.
We gave them all our love,
they raided all our dreams
and ate up all our jam,
and left us just like that;
laughed all down the road.

Our kids have just left home.
And oh the sweet relief,
come,let's postpone our grief
and please answer the phone.

They're coming three o'clock?
And staying for the night?
Where did we go right?